Th

Chartered Psy
illustrator Nick
to create a playful and uplifting guide to positive thinking. Sam has spent many years helping people take positive action in their lives by making self-help strategies engaging, practical and easy to use.

Read the psychologist's top tips and integrate them into your happy married life.

Enjoy the journey!

To:

With positive thoughts from:

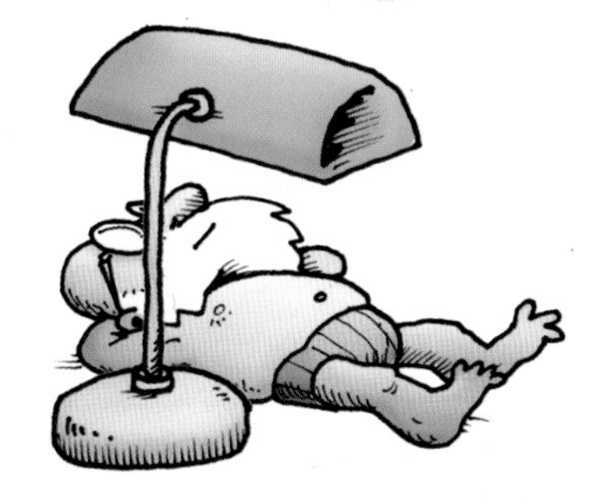

Super Laughter

Regular laughter with your partner
is the best medicine to keep a
marriage full of life and excitement.

Laughter will release feel-good
chemicals into your brain that will
add value to any experience.

Make a list of activities
to enjoy together and share
the magic of laughter.

Try watching live comedy,
sharing funny stories and
spending time with friends
who make you laugh.

Common Ground

A successful marriage is predominantly based on two people who share similar and complementary values.

Whenever you go through a rough patch, spend quality time together reminding yourself of what you have in common.

Use your evenings together to talk about shared interests and topics that engage both of you.

Positive Communication

Most of human communication is non-verbal. Body language and voice tonality is more important than the words themselves.

When you communicate with your partner ensure that you focus on the delivery rather than the words of your message.

Eye contact, smiles and welcoming body language are essential.

Open-Up

Everyone has fears and
insecurities and sometimes it
isn't easy to talk about them.

In your marriage, ensure that you
take the courage to open up!

Although this process
often feels uncomfortable,
afterwards you will
invariably experience a
sense of liberation and freedom.

You will also feel closer
to your partner.

The Feel Good Factor

Spend time getting yourself into a resourceful state before spending quality time with your partner.

Thinking about happy memories, taking a few minutes to focus your mind on the present moment and actively smiling are some simple actions that will strengthen your shared experience with your partner.

Emotions are contagious, so if you are feeling good it is likely that it will spread to those around you!

Magical Appreciation

When you are close to someone
it is easy to fall into the trap
of taking them for granted.

When we start expecting things
from our partner it becomes harder
to appreciate their love and kindness.

If you expect nothing from your
interactions with your partner,
it will mean so much more when
they shower you with love
and affection!

Accept The Lows

In all human relationships there
are inevitable ups and downs.

When you are feeling sad,
try not to fight your emotions.

Battling against how you
feel will worsen your mood
and rub off on your partner.

Learn to accept the negative
by surrendering to the lows.

You will pass through
the negative more swiftly
and be ready to enjoy
the highs together.

Not So Smart Phones

Modern technology can damage the quality of the time spent with your partner. Smartphones are the front runner for this!

When you're with your partner, resist the temptation to fiddle with your phone. Keep your focus on them to ensure that you communicate in a positive way.

Love Or Adrenaline?

Seek out daring and exciting activities that will get your heart racing.

Psychologists have evidence that shows when our heart rate is elevated and we are with our partners we are likely to ascribe the change in our bodies not to the adventurous activity but to the feeling we have for our loved one.

Forgiveness

One of the most important processes in any loving relationship is forgiveness.

We all make mistakes from time to time, especially when we are married.

The breakdown of a significant proportion of relationships is due to an inability to forgive.

Practising forgiveness on a daily basis will improve the quality of your marriage and contribute to your overall well-being.

Remember to forgive yourself as well as others!

Special Support

To make your marriage even more positive, learn from other couples and share experiences.

During tough times, a sense of isolation can worsen negative thinking.

Nine times out of ten when you share your troubles with other couples you will realise that you are not the only ones.

Mix It Up!

When you are in a long-term relationship it is easy to get into the habit of following the same routines. Habits are difficult to break, especially the ones that you have practised for years!

Variety is the spice of life. Set the goal of doing something different together every week.

Sit down together and come up with appropriate new and exciting ideas. Think about joining a dance class, going to a new restaurant or travelling to new places.

Great Giving

One of the most rewarding benefits
of a long-term relationship
is being able to contribute and
add value to your partner's life.

Being of service to your partner
in loving ways is essential
to a happy marriage.

If you feel that you don't contribute
to the life of the person you love, it is
unlikely that you will feel fulfilled in
the relationship. The more you are able
to give in a long-term relationship
the more you will receive!

Personal Space

However amazing your marriage, it is also important that you allow each other personal space.

A healthy marriage should be supportive of individual goals and ambitions, as well as joint ones.

Encouraging each other to fulfil personal dreams and goals will strengthen your marriage.

Happy Choices

In many people's lives,
marriage is the big goal.

When so much expectation and
build-up is placed on the process
of getting married, pressure
is created to feel happy and
fulfilled the moment your get there!

However, if you weren't happy before
you got married, nothing will change
once you are.

Achieving long-lasting happiness
is an internal shift, and it is not
something that happens by
changing your life on the outside.

Quality Not Quantity

The hectic lives we lead can place a strain on the time we can spend with our partner.

Remind yourself that it is not the amount of time that you spend with each other, but the quality that is important.

A short amount of time full of love and happiness is much healthier than a lengthy period lacking in genuine emotion.

Positive Spaces

The quality of your living space
is an important component
in creating a happy marriage.

Fill your home with positive
objects that will trigger
happy memories and emotions.

Photos of loved ones, mementos
from past holidays and symbols
of your special achievements
will contribute to making your
shared space a happy
and healthy place to be.

Grow Together

Marriage is not so much a state,
as an evolution.

Both of you will change and
develop new goals and priorities
in your relationship.

See marriage as a space
in which you can learn and
explore life together.

Take On The Challenge!

In some ways, marriage is like being part of a small team.

If something goes wrong in any team, it is important not to look for blame.

Tackle problems together and see them as a joint challenge to overcome.

When problems are shared you will become more focused on solving them.

Love Yourself

You can only be held responsible for your own wellbeing and no one else's. Although you can choose to behave in ways that will support those around you, inevitably you cannot control how someone feels.

In your marriage it is important that each of you take ownership for your own well-being. If you rely on the other as a source of happiness, the likely consequence will be that you will constantly feel as if your needs are not being met and that something is lacking. Love yourself first and everything in your marriage will seem much sweeter.

The Pocket Psychologist™
Other Titles in the Series

Published by Mindsport Ltd in 2012
Printed in China

Mindsport Ltd
72 Prince Street, Bristol, BS1 4QD, United Kingdom
www.MyPositiveUniverse.com